❖ GREAT LITTLE COOK BOOKS ❖

Italian
COOKING

Italy is a country for dreaming...

of lush, green and barren, rocky landscapes, of a dark blue sea with fine golden sand, of lively, friendly people, of sparkling wine and, of course, of wonderful Italian food.

This book has been designed to give your dreams some 'bite' and to make them come true. Read and cook until you have had your fill of delicious antipasti, tasty soups, wonderful polenta and rice dishes, sophisticated vegetables, superb fish and seafood, traditional meat dishes and melt-in-the mouth desserts.

AURA

CONTENTS

Meat dishes 48

Desserts 56

Recipes and Index 62

Regions are trumps

L'Italia è un paese senza gli Italiani say our Italian friends, by which they mean that Italy is a country that does not have any 'real' Italians. Although the ancient city-states were united into a single kingdom over one hundred years ago, regional differences have persisted very strongly into the present-day republic. Italy is the land of the Milanese, the Venetians, the Florentines, the Romans, the Sicilians and the Neapolitans.

Other European countries are no strangers to a degree of rivalry between respective regions. In Italy, however, these differences exist even between neighbouring towns and villages within the same region. This demonstrates the strength of the influence of centuries of a constantly changing history on the hearts and minds of the Italian people.

The patriotism of the small town

The Italian word *campanalísmo* implies that every citizen is proud of the church tower of his own home town and considers *his* home town to be so beautiful that it cannot possibly have a rival. This 'petty patriotism' may sometimes make life a little difficult for politicians, but it has had a wonderfully positive effect on Italian cuisine. For generations, families have cooked in accordance with ancient traditions. The inhabitants of the various regions swear to the excellence of their own local dishes, while quite consistently rejecting the dishes of their neighbours. Which dishes are the best is the subject for vigorous debate everywhere in Italy. This is why such a culinary profusion and variety have developed and been preserved in Italy in a way that hardly any other country in the world can match.

'Campanalísmo' – literally, pride in the church tower of your home town – also means being proud of the heritage, including the culinary heritage, of your own region. This is why numerous regional specialities have been preserved in their original form and are still prepared today in accordance with ancient tradition.

Bologna, the fat and Tuscany, the simple

In the South Tyrol and the Trentino, the influence of the ancient Danube monarchy on regional cuisine is immediately apparent. Barley soup, bacon dumplings and the famous local doughnuts sit side-by-side on the same menu with *gnocchi, minestrone* and *ravioli*. Bologna, the capital of Emilia-Romagna, is not called *la grassa* – the fat city – in vain, because in this region of Italy, cooks do not use butter and cream sparingly when it comes to preparing *lasagne al forno, cannelloni* or even only a *ragù alla bolognese* for a spaghetti dish.

In neighbouring Tuscany, on the other hand, they prefer their food to be less rich. The Tuscans prefer to cook rather more simply, almost sparingly, and yet – or perhaps for that very reason – Tuscan cuisine has a character as noble as the Tuscan landscape. The secret of that character lies in the fact that few, but only the very best, ingredients are used in any dish, Tuscans also fully understand the art of enhancing those ingredients with fresh herbs.

Fifty variations on the theme of risotto

In the Veneto and in Lombardy they proudly boast of at least fifty variations on the theme of *risotto. La polenta* – delicious slices of thick-set cornmeal – is served there only as an accompaniment to fish and meat dishes. In Piedmont, on the other hand, polenta is used in close combination with tasty sauces, local cheeses and truffles, which are placed on top of it and baked in the oven to produce delicious dishes.

Neapolitans, however, know of polenta only through hearsay and they totally reject the notion of even trying risotto. Of course, this does not prevent them, once a year at Easter, from baking a large number of wonderful tarts from the otherwise despised rice. These are then shared freely with numerous relatives and friends. The *spaghetti al pomodoro* of this region, just like the *pizza alla napoletana,* have, meanwhile, become part of the repertoire of almost every restaurant on the Italian peninsula, even if they do not always stick to the original recipe when it comes to preparing the sauce.

The little devil peperoncino

The natives of the Abruzzi spice their sauces so generously with peperoncino that the colour of their food owes more to this variety of hot red chilli than to the tomatoes they also use copiously. It is no wonder that they call it *diavoletto* (little devil). It is as red as the chasm of hell and as fiery as Lucifer himself, say the peasants. They keep warm from within by using peperoncino when, in the winter months, their log fires do not provide sufficient warmth. It is advisable to treat this hot spice with care.

Tied decoratively together in a long plait, these hot little red peppers look extremely attractive hung on the outside walls of people's houses to dry in the sunshine.

Highly decorative to look at, these little red peppers are so fiery hot that they are called 'diavoletto' – little devils – by the people of the Abruzzi.

A passion for pasta and vegetables

Neapolitans do not consider that they have eaten a meal unless they have consumed their beloved *pasta*. Consequently, they have been nicknamed *mangiamaccheroni* (macaroni eaters). They get their own back on the neighbouring Pugliesi (Apulia) by calling them *mangiafoglie* (leaf eaters), which implies vegetable eaters. Indeed, many excellent vegetables specialities originate from Apulia. It was there, for example, that the delicious *calzone* (a covered or folded-over pizza) was created by taking the simple, classic pizza and adding a lavish vegetable filling.

The people of Liguria also have a preference for lots of vegetables. Even the regional noodle dish of Liguria is green, although, in this case, it owes its colour to the generous use of fresh basil. The basil of Liguria is said to have the best flavour of any. This is why the Genoese always take a supply of the herb with them whenever they leave home.

Italian vegetable dishes are superb. This should not really be a surprise when you think about the rich variety of fresh, sun-ripened vegetables available. Fennel, for example, is served throughout the country in many different ways.

Fresh fish

In the area around the ancient sea port of Genoa, the Ligurians know exactly how to treat their superb *frutti di mare* (seafood). The reputation enjoyed among gourmets of the many fabulous fish and other seafood dishes results not only from their delicious taste, but also from the variety of fresh seafood on offer everywhere in such abundance in the fish markets there.

Proud Sardinians and 'sweet' Sicilians

The Sardinians, despite being surrounded by the sea, have never taken fishing seriously. They are a proud, self-confident people, who are still very much set in their traditional ways and customs. Neither foreign invaders in the course of their history, nor the flood of foreign tourists in modern times has changed the way of life of those Sardinians who live inland. Their cuisine is simple, even archaic – both as regards the content and the preparation of their dishes.

Sicilian cuisine, on the other hand, has skilfully integrated the many foreign influences experienced in the course of the island's varied history. Arab and Spanish influences are particularly apparent in the lavish recipes for desserts. No other region is as rich in delicious pastries and sweets: one glance through the window of any patisserie is enough to make you forget any thought of dieting. Another dish reflecting foreign influence is *cucusu*, a cousin of North African couscous.

Colourful markets

To ensure a healthy, balanced diet and a thoroughly appetizing meal, Sicilian housewives prepare a vast range of delicious vegetable dishes. The ingredients can be obtained on the island throughout the year in rich abundance. Nowhere else in Italy – and, possibly, the rest of Europe – are the markets so full of colour, fragrance, choice and life as they are here.

A tourist who has visited Monreale, Cefalu and Selenunte, but who has neglected to visit a Sicilian market on his travels will have missed out on an important part of Sicilian culture.

It should now be obvious that Italian cuisine is as colourful and varied as the Italian landscape. The wide variety of regional specialities makes it almost impossible to decide what to include and what to leave out.

Italians are born gourmets

There are hundreds of different opinions among Italians as to *what* to eat, but total agreement as to *how*. For every Italian is a born gourmet and knows almost instinctively whether any particular dish has been prepared in the best possible way. This means that all ingredients must be of the best quality, the herbs and spices should be well balanced and the cooking time calculated precisely. The farmer's wife in the Abruzzi makes her *sugo al pomodoro* with the same care and attention as the cook employed in a Roman palazzo. If you were a guest at a special feast provided by an agricultural worker, you would be no more able to do justice to the wealth of different dishes on offer than to do justice to the many courses offered in the richest house in the land.

Every visitor to an Italian market is delighted by the, colour, freshness and immense variety of what is on offer. Some of the unfamiliar fruit and vegetables will arouse the traveller's curiosity and entice him to try them. The recipes in this book also provide many delightful incentives to do so, too.

The fruits of one of the oldest cultivated plants on earth, the olive tree: its oil, ranging from deep green to golden-yellow in colour, depending on the region where it is produced, is an essential part of Italian cuisine.

Olive oil is number one!

Oil, butter, pork fat and bacon are all used for frying and other types of cooking, depending on the region in which any particular dish is made. For salads, however, only the best olive oil is good enough – and the Italians dress their salads according to ancient rules.

They use oil like a spendthrift, vinegar like a miser and salt and pepper like a sage. Then they mix the salad like a madman – that is, over and over again. They buy their favourite cheeses, such as Parmesan or pecorino, in one piece and grate or shave them freshly over the salad. They buy their herbs as fresh as possible from the market. Marjoram, thyme, oregano, rosemary and sage, however, also keep their taste when dried. The fact that vitamins are often lost through long cooking times is of no great concern to an Italian cook. Fresh salads and plenty of fruit for dessert easily make up for any loss of vitamins in cooked dishes.

The best-quality olive oil is extra virgin, which is from the first cold pressing and has a maximum acidity of one per cent. It is quite expensive, but well worth buying for making salad dressings. Virgin olive oil is slightly more acid and not quite so expensive. Oil simply labelled pure is usually refined and heat-treated and, therefore, lacks both character and flavour.

Pasta

Pastas are among the most important Italian foodstuffs. There are a vast number of different varieties for a good reason: not every pasta can absorb a particular sauce as well as another. Pastas are boiled until they are *al dente*, which means that they are tender, but still firm to the bite.

The same technique is applied to cooking fine vegetables. Green beans, cauliflower, broccoli, fennel and courgettes are served when they still have 'bite' to them. When fresh tomatoes are no longer in season in Italy, they use canned ones to make their sauces because these give the dishes a guaranteed powerful flavour and an intense colour.

Long pasta: spaghetti, tagliarini, taglioni, vermicelli, tagliatelle, maccheroni, fettuccine, linguine, mafaldini, pappardelle.
Pasta shapes: fusilli, farfalle, orecchiette, conchiglie, lumache, rotele, eliche, penne, tubetti, cresti di gallo, tripolini, ziti, campanelle, rigatoni, spirali, garganelle.
Pasta for soups: stellete, conchigliete, anellini, ditalini.
Stuffed pasta: ravioli, tortelloni, agnolotti, cappelletti, cannelloni, caramellone.

Mangiare in compagnia

Food and drink play an important part in every Italian family. Old and young join each other around the table and not merely to satisfy their hunger. Eating together is very important to Italians, for talking to one's neighbour at the dining table even takes priority over the pleasure of eating. Italians really do communicate with each other – a rite which even the hectic nature of modern times cannot spoil.

From antipasto to espresso

An Italian meal begins with the *antipasto*, a starter, which often just consists of home-made salami and a few olives. *Minestre* (soups), *paste* (pastas served with a variety of sauces), *risotti* (rice dishes) or *gnocchi* (dumplings made from potatoes, semolina or cornmeal) make up the first course, depending on the custom of the region. These serve to take the edge off one's hunger. The *secondo* follows: fish, meat, and egg dishes are served with fresh salad or cooked vegetables. The diners break their bread into pieces and mop up any remaining sauce. Generally speaking, cheese and fruit finish the meal. A bottle of light, dry country wine and a jug of iced water also belong on the table, as does a basket of slices of white bread. A strong, fragrant *espresso* at the end of the meal stirs the guest again to new life.

The festive menu and what to drink with it

In Italy, there are very few differences between a festive meal and an everyday meal. The starters and the first course are more lavish and two main courses are often served instead of one. The well-filled basket of fruit makes way for delicious desserts. Before the meal, guests are offered an aperitif and at the end a *digestivo*, a herb liqueur, or a *grappa*. A *fernet* may also be offered to soothe the stomach.

Who does not dream of living here? Tuscany is one of the gourmet regions of Italy. The cuisine, like the landscape, is simple, unspoilt and in harmony with nature.

Carpaccio

MARINATED FILLET OF BEEF

For guests

Serves 4
200 g/7 oz raw fillet of beef, cut into wafer-thin slices
salt
freshly ground white pepper
30 ml/2 tablespoons lemon juice
4 tablespoons extra virgin olive oil
½ bunch fresh parsley
50 g/2 oz Parmesan cheese
1 lemon
fresh white bread, to serve

Approximately per portion:
810 kJ/190 kcal
15 g protein
14 g fat
3 g carbohydrate

- Approximate preparation time: 20–25 minutes

1. Arrange the slices of beef on 4 individual serving plates.

2. Stir a pinch of salt and a little pepper into the lemon juice. Add the oil and stir vigorously until well blended. Pour the dressing evenly over the meat, cover the plates with clear film and set aside to marinate at room temperature for 5–10 minutes.

3. Pull the parsley leaves off the stems and chop finely.

4. Just before serving, shave wafer-thin slices from the Parmesan cheese, using a vegetable peeler, and scatter sparingly over the meat. Cut the lemon into 8 slices. Garnish the carpaccio with the slices of lemon and the parsley and serve immediately with fresh white bread.

Cipolline in insalata

ONION SALAD

Inexpensive

Serves 4
salt
750 g/1 lb 10 oz shallots
120 ml/4 fl oz double cream
60 ml/4 tablespoons mayonnaise
freshly ground white pepper
1 lemon
fresh parsley sprigs, to garnish

Approximately per portion:
1,100 kJ/260 kcal
4 g protein
21 g fat
17 g carbohydrate

- Approximate preparation time: 1 hour

1. Bring a pan of lightly salted water to the boil. Add the shallots, cover and simmer over a low heat for 20–30 minutes. Drain and set aside to cool completely.

2. Lightly beat the cream, stir in the mayonnaise and season to taste with salt and pepper.

3. Arrange the shallots on a flat serving dish and pour over the sauce. Cut the lemon into slices and arrange around the plate. Garnish with the parsley sprigs and serve.

Variations

Cipolline lesse alla veronese
Simmer 750 g/1 lb 10 oz medium-size, white onions in lightly salted boiling water over a low heat. Drain, then cut into quarters lengthways. Put the quartered pieces into a salad bowl and sprinkle with fresh or dried oregano. Season with salt and pepper and drizzle over 75 ml/ 5 tablespoons extra virgin olive oil.

Cipolline alla siciliana
Simmer 750 g/1 lb 10 oz small new onions in lightly salted boiling water over a low heat until they are just tender, but still firm to the bite. Drain well. Heat 90 ml/ 6 tablespoons olive oil in a large, shallow pan, add the onions in a single layer and fry over a low heat, turning frequently, until they are light golden brown all over. Sprinkle over 5 ml/1 teaspoon sugar, then pour in 120 ml/4 fl oz balsamic vinegar. Season to taste with salt and pepper. Cover and simmer over a very low heat for about 10 minutes. Remove the saucepan from the heat and set aside to cool completely.

Above: Carpaccio, a famous classic dish, is always a great success.
Below: Cipolline in insalata is a very simple, but sophisticated, starter.

Pizza alla romana

PIZZA WITH TOMATOES, MOZZARELLA CHEESE AND ANCHOVIES

Inexpensive

When Italians celebrate a festival in the southern countryside, they often serve pizza as a starter. As ovens vary considerably, it is worth knowing that you can also bake the pizza at 230–240°C/450–475°F/ Gas 8–9.

Serves 4
For the dough:
20 g/¾ oz yeast
about 120 ml/4 fl oz lukewarm water
300 g/11 oz plain flour
salt
30 ml/2 tablespoons olive oil, plus extra for greasing

For the topping:
400 g/14 oz beef tomatoes
5 fresh basil sprigs
4–5 anchovy fillets
300 g/11 oz mozzarella cheese
freshly ground black pepper
salt
45 ml/3 tablespoons freshly grated pecorino cheese
60 ml/4 tablespoons olive oil

Approximately per portion:
2,600 kJ/620 kcal
29 g protein
32 g fat
53 g carbohydrate

- Approximate preparation time: 2¼ hours

1. Crumble the yeast, then stir it into 30 ml/2 tablespoons of the lukewarm water until smooth. Sift the flour with a pinch of salt on to a work surface. Make a hollow in the centre, pour in the yeast mixture and draw in the flour with your fingertips to cover. Leave the dough mixture to rise until cracks show on the surface. This takes about 15 minutes. Gradually pour the remaining lukewarm water into the hollow, while working the flour from the inside to the outside with your fingertips.

2. Knead the dough until it is smooth and elastic. Shape it into a ball, make a crossways cut in the top, dust with flour and cover with a clean tea cloth. Leave to prove for about 1 hour, until the dough has doubled in size.

3. Meanwhile, blanch the tomatoes in boiling water for 1–2 minutes. Drain, skin, cut in half and seed. Cut the tomato flesh lengthways into strips and set aside in a colander to drain.

4. Cut the basil leaves into thin strips. Chop the anchovy fillets. Thinly slice the mozzarella.

5. Preheat the oven to 220°C/ 425°F/Gas 7. Brush a baking sheet well with olive oil.

6. Knock back the dough and vigorously knead in the olive oil. Roll out the dough on the prepared baking sheet. Arrange the tomatoes, mozzarella and anchovies on top. Season with pepper and a little salt, then sprinkle over the pecorino and basil. Drizzle with the olive oil.

7. Bake the pizza in the oven for 20–25 minutes, until the top is golden and the cheese has melted.

Variations

Pizza quattro stagioni
Cover one quarter of the pizza with drained canned clams or other shellfish, one quarter with olives and capers, one quarter with artichoke hearts and one quarter with tomatoes and thinly sliced mozzarella cheese. Season with salt and pepper and drizzle with olive oil.

Pizza alla marinara
Cover the pizza base with 500 g/ 1¼ lb tomatoes prepared according to the recipe. Top with 90 g/3½ oz chopped, stoned black olives, 5 chopped anchovies and 15 ml/1 tablespoon capers. Season with salt, pepper and chopped fresh oregano. Drizzle generously with olive oil.

One look at this and who could stop themselves from wanting to cook and eat it? This pizza alla romana not only looks delicious – it tastes wonderful, too!

Mozzarella e pomodori

MOZZARELLA AND TOMATOES

Quick

This very simple, but quite delicious, starter is quick to prepare, but it does require the very best-quality ingredients. Buy genuine Italian mozzarella cheese if at all possible.

Serves 4
600 g/1 lb 5 oz firm, ripe beef tomatoes
300 g/11 oz mozzarella cheese
fresh basil sprigs
about 120 ml/4 fl oz extra virgin olive oil, to serve

Approximately per portion:
2,000 kJ/480 kcal
17 g protein
44 g fat
5 g carbohydrate

- Approximate preparation time: 15 minutes

1. Cut the tomatoes into slices about 5 ml/¼ inch thick. Drain the mozzarella cheese and cut into thin, even slices.

2. Arrange the slices of tomato and mozzarella cheese alternately on a round serving dish so that they overlap slightly.

3. Pull the basil leaves off the stems and tear any large ones into pieces. Scatter the basil over the tomatoes and cheese.

4. Serve the salad with a jug of olive oil, so that everyone can serve themselves.

Variation

Insalata di pomodori e mozzarella
Cut 6 small, firm salad tomatoes into equal slices and arrange on individual plates. Divide 400 g/14 oz diced mozzarella cheese, 5 chopped anchovy fillets and 24 stoned black olives between the plates. Sprinkle generously with small or coarsely torn fresh basil leaves. Mix together 75 ml/5 tablespoons extra virgin olive oil, a pinch of salt and freshly ground black pepper and drizzle the dressing over the salad.

Sardine marinate

SARDINES IN A MARINADE

Sophisticated

Serves 4
2 x 120 g/4¼ oz cans sardines in oil, skinned and boned
1 bunch fresh mint
1 bunch fresh parsley
2 anchovy fillets
60 ml/4 tablespoons balsamic vinegar
30 ml/2 tablespoons extra virgin olive oil
salt
freshly ground white pepper
½ lemon
crusty white bread, to serve

Approximately per portion:
510 kJ/120 kcal
12 g protein
7 g fat
3 g carbohydrate

- Approximate preparation time: 1¼ hours

1. With a sharp knife, cut the sardines along their length, so that the fillets can be opened wide.

2. Arrange the fillets in a fan shape on a round serving dish.

3. Reserve 3 mint sprigs for the garnish. Remove the stalks from the parsley and the remaining mint and finely chop the leaves. Finely chop the anchovy fillets.

4. Mix together the chopped mint, parsley, anchovies, balsamic vinegar and olive oil. Season to taste with salt and pepper. Drizzle over the sardine fillets.

5. Cut off a 1 cm/½ inch thick slice of lemon. Using a small knife, cut out serrations in the rind to make a decorative edge. Place the lemon slice in the centre of the sardines. Garnish with the remaining mint leaves.

6. Set the sardines aside in the refrigerator to marinate for about 1 hour, then serve at room temperature with slices of crusty white bread.

Above: Mozzarella e pomodori
Below: Sardine marinate

Minestrone al pesto

THICK VEGETABLE SOUP WITH PESTO

Rather time-consuming

This wonderful vegetable soup has its origins in peasant cookery and even today, housewives are still using their imagination to make up their own soups with fresh vegetables in summer or dried pulses with a generous addition of olive oil or chopped bacon in winter. This recipe is, therefore, a kind of summer and winter liaison.

Serves 4
115 g/4 oz dried borlotti or haricot beans
2 onions
2 courgettes
2 carrots
2 potatoes
½ small Savoy cabbage
4 tomatoes
60 ml/4 tablespoons olive oil
1.2 litres/2 pints meat or vegetable stock
115–150 g/4–5 oz small pasta shapes
salt
freshly ground black pepper
freshly grated Parmesan cheese, to serve

For the pesto:
1 bunch fresh basil
1 garlic clove
salt
freshly ground white pepper
7.5 ml/1½ teaspoons pine nuts
20 g/¾ oz freshly grated pecorino cheese
50 ml/2 fl oz olive oil

Approximately per portion:
1,600 kJ/380 kcal
18 g protein
12 g fat
52 g carbohydrate

- Approximate preparation time: 10 hours
- Soaking time: about 8 hours

1. Put the beans in a bowl and add just enough cold water to cover. Set aside to soak overnight.

2. Finely chop the onions. Dice the courgettes, carrots and potatoes. Shred the cabbage.

3. Blanch the tomatoes in boiling water for 1–2 minutes. Drain, skin and cut into quarters.

4. Heat the oil in a large saucepan. Add the onions and fry for 2–3 minutes, until soft. Add the courgettes, carrots, potatoes, cabbage and tomatoes. Cover and cook over a low heat for about 10 minutes.

5. Meanwhile, bring the stock to the boil in a saucepan. Drain the beans and discard the soaking water. Add the beans to the pan of vegetables. Pour in the stock and simmer for about 1 hour 20 minutes, until the beans are tender and nearly cooked.

6. Meanwhile, make the pesto. Pull the basil leaves off the stalks. Crush the garlic. Pound the basil with a pinch of salt in a mortar with a pestle. Add white pepper to taste and the garlic and pine kernels. Pound to form a smooth paste. Gradually add the cheese and the olive oil, drop by drop. Continue to pound until the pesto becomes creamy.

7. Add the pasta to the saucepan and cook, uncovered, for a further 10 minutes, until the pasta is tender, but still firm to the bite. Stir in the pesto. Season to taste with salt and pepper and serve immediately with freshly grated Parmesan cheese.

Tip

Why not serve garlic bread with this minestrone al pesto? Toast slices of white bread and vigorously rub with the cut side of a halved garlic clove. This turns this dish into a light meal.

If you are in a hurry, you can leave out the pesto and simply sprinkle freshly grated pecorino or Parmesan cheese over the minestrone.

Zuppa pavese

MEAT SOUP WITH BREAD AND EGG

Quick

This is a delicious, sophisticated soup, but only if the best-quality meat and absolutely fresh eggs are used.

Serves 4
1 litre/1¾ pints meat stock
50 g/2 oz butter
4 slices white bread
50 g/2 oz freshly grated Parmesan cheese
4 eggs
salt

Approximately per portion:
1,600 kJ/380 kcal
20 g protein
29 g fat
11 g carbohydrate

- Approximate preparation time: 20 minutes

Tip

To make meat stock, put a sliced carrot, sliced onion, chopped celery stick, chopped leek, bay leaf, 2–3 cloves, 1.5 ml/¼ teaspoon black peppercorns, 250 g/9 oz beef bones, 15 ml/1 tablespoon salt and 1.2 litres/2 pints cold water in a saucepan. Bring to the boil and skim off the scum. Cover and simmer for 2–4 hours. Strain and set aside to cool.

1. Heat the stock in a pan almost to boiling point. Meanwhile, melt the butter in a large frying pan. Add the slices of bread and fry on both sides until golden brown, so that the outsides are crispy, but the insides remain soft.

2. Put the slices of fried bread in the base of 4 individual soup bowls. Sprinkle over half the Parmesan cheese.

3. Break 1 egg on each slice of fried bread, making sure that the yoke does not break. (It is not so authentic, but the eggs will be less runny if you poach or fry them for a short time and then place on the fried bread.) Lightly season each egg with salt and sprinkle over the remaining cheese.

4. Carefully pour the hot stock into each soup bowl, down the side, and serve immediately.

Pancotto al modo mio

BREAD SOUP WITH TOMATOES

Rather time-consuming

This popular soup is a recent successor to the Tuscan *pappa col pomodoro*, a meal for poor people who live in the countryside. As a result of the long cooking time and frequent stirring, the bread virtually disintegrates. What remains is an elegant soup with a creamy consistency, which can form part of any menu.

Serves 4
2 garlic cloves
1 celery stick
1 bunch fresh parsley
1 bunch fresh basil
400 g/14 oz can tomatoes
90 ml/6 tablespoons olive oil
1.2 litres/2 pints meat stock
about 150 g/5 oz day-old white bread, cut into thin slices
salt
freshly ground black pepper
50 g/2 oz freshly grated Parmesan cheese, to serve

Approximately per portion:
1,300 kJ/310 kcal
12 g protein
18 g fat
24 g carbohydrate

- Approximate preparation time: 2 hours

1. Finely chop the garlic and celery. Pull the parsley and basil leaves off the stalks and finely chop. Rub the tomatoes, together with their can juice through a strainer.

2. Heat the oil in a large saucepan. Add the garlic, celery, parsley and basil and fry over a low heat for about 5 minutes. Add the tomatoes, cover and simmer over a very low heat for about 15 minutes.

3. Meanwhile, bring the stock to the boil. Add the bread to the pan of vegetables and cook, stirring constantly, for 1 minute, then pour in the boiling stock.

4. Cover and cook over a low heat, stirring frequently, for about 25 minutes. Season to taste with salt and pepper. Serve immediately with the grated cheese.

Minestra di funghi e verdura

MUSHROOM AND VEGETABLE SOUP

Inexpensive

Serves 4
1.2 litres/2 pints meat stock
1 large onion
200 g/7 oz carrots
3 celery sticks
3 beef tomatoes
250 g/9 oz mushrooms
4 slices white bread
15–30 ml/1–2 tablespoons olive oil
salt
freshly ground white pepper
50 g/2 oz freshly grated Parmesan cheese, to serve

Approximately per portion:
900 kJ/210 kcal
12 g protein
10 g fat
19 g carbohydrate

- Approximate preparation time: 1 hour 5 minutes

1. Bring the stock to the boil in a large saucepan.

2. Thinly slice the onions and push out into rings. Thinly slice the carrots. Cut the celery into 3 cm/1¼ inch long pieces.

3. Blanch the tomatoes in boiling water for 1–2 minutes. Drain, skin and chop coarsely.

4. Add the onions, carrots, celery and tomatoes to the stock, cover, lower the heat and simmer for about 45 minutes.

5. Thinly slice the mushrooms, add to the saucepan, cover and simmer over a low heat for a further 20 minutes.

6. Toast the slices of bread. Put 1 slice of toast into the base of 4 individual soup bowls and drizzle over the olive oil.

7. Season the soup with salt and pepper to taste and pour into a warmed tureen. At the table, ladle very hot soup over the slices of bread and hand the Parmesan cheese separately.

Zuppa di spinaci

SPRING SOUP WITH SPINACH

Easy to make

Serves 4
600 g/1 lb 5 oz young spinach leaves
50 g/2 oz butter
1 litre/1¾ pints meat or vegetable stock
2 eggs
105 ml/7 tablespoons freshly grated Parmesan cheese
salt
freshly ground white pepper
freshly grated nutmeg
2 slices white bread

Approximately per portion:
1,600 kJ/380 kcal
21 g protein
31 g fat
7 g carbohydrate

- Approximate preparation time: 50 minutes

1. Remove any coarse stems from the spinach. Put the leaves in a saucepan, cover and cook over a high heat, in only the water clinging to them after washing, until just wilted. Shake the pan frequently. Drain and set aside to cool. Squeeze out any excess water, then chop finely.

2. Melt 15 g/½ oz of the butter in a frying pan. Add the spinach and cook over a low heat, stirring frequently, for about 5 minutes.

3. Bring the stock to the boil in a large saucepan.

4. In a mixing bowl, beat together the eggs and 45 ml/3 tablespoons of the Parmesan cheese until thoroughly combined. Mix in the spinach and season to taste with salt, pepper and nutmeg.

5. Dice the slices of bread. Melt the remaining butter in a frying pan. Add the bread and fry, stirring and turning frequently, until golden brown. Divide the bread cubes between 4 individual soup bowls.

6. Add the spinach mixture to the boiling stock, beating vigorously with a whisk. Remove the pan from the heat, cover and set aside to stand for about 5 minutes.

7. Pour the soup into a warmed tureen. At the table, ladle the soup over the bread cubes and hand the remaining cheese separately.

Above: Minestra di funghi e verdura
Below: Zuppa di spinaci

Polenta

(BASIC RECIPE)

Easy to make

Serves 4
1.2 litres/2 pints water
15 ml/1 tablespoon salt
50 g/2 oz coarsely ground polenta or cornmeal flour

Approximately per portion:
1,200 kJ/290 kcal
8 g protein
1 g fat
64 g carbohydrate

- Approximate preparation time: 1 hour

1. Put the water and salt in a large saucepan and bring to the boil.

2. Slowly tip in the polenta or cornmeal flour, beating constantly with the whisk to ensure that no lumps form. Cook over a low heat, stirring constantly with a wooden spoon, for about 45 minutes. The meal will gradually swell to form a firm mixture.

3. Turn the mixture out on to a dampened dish or into an oiled roasting tin, smooth the surface, cover and set aside to cool.

4. Cut the polenta into slices.

5. The slices can be used freshly boiled, fried in butter or grilled to accompany a dish.

Gnocchi di polenta al gorgonzola

DUMPLINGS MADE FROM POLENTA WITH GORGONZOLA

Sophisticated

Serves 4
1.2 litres/2 pints water
15 ml/1 tablespoon salt
350 g/12 oz coarsely ground polenta or cornmeal flour
90 g/3½ oz butter, plus extra for greasing
185 g/6½ oz gorgonzola cheese
90 g/3½ oz cooked ham
90 g/3½ oz freshly grated Parmesan cheese
60–75 ml/4–5 tablespoons double cream
30 ml/2 tablespoons finely chopped fresh parsley

Approximately per portion:
3,600 kJ/860 kcal
311 g protein
52 g fat
65 g carbohydrate

- Approximate preparation time: 1¼ hours

1. Make the polenta according to the basic recipe (left) with the water, salt and polenta or cornmeal flour.

2. Grease an ovenproof dish with butter. Preheat the oven to 200°C/400°F/Gas 6.

3. Dice the gorgonzola cheese and the ham.

4. Using a wet tablespoon, scoop gnocchi out of the cooked polenta, shaping them into neat dumplings. Arrange a layer of gnocchi in the prepared dish, scatter over the gorgonzola cheese and dot with half the butter. Make a second layer of gnocchi, scatter over the ham and sprinkle over the Parmesan cheese. Make a third layer of gnocchi, dot with the remaining butter, then pour over the cream. Sprinkle over the chopped, fresh parsley.

5. Bake in the middle of the oven for 30 minutes, until golden brown.

Variation

Polenta alla pancetta

Thinly slice 2 onions and push out into rings. Dice 150 g/5 oz pancetta or smoked streaky bacon. Melt 30 ml/2 tablespoons pork dripping or heat 30 ml/2 table-spoons olive oil in a frying pan. Add the pancetta or bacon and the onions and fry over a low heat until the onion rings are soft, but not brown. Spoon over the gnocchi, sprinkle with grated Parmesan cheese to taste and bake in the oven, as above.

Tip

Coarsely ground polenta or cornmeal flour becomes firm more easily during cooking and has a grainier taste. However, if you do not like stirring for such a long time, use one that is ground more finely.

Above: Gnocchi di polenta al gorgonzola
Below: Polenta

Risotto alla golosa

RISOTTO WITH MEAT AND VEGETABLES

Sophisticated

Serves 4
2 onions
2 red peppers
250 g/9 oz boneless shoulder of veal
30 ml/2 tablespoons olive oil
25 g/1 oz butter
salt
freshly ground white pepper
about 1 litre/1¾ pints meat or vegetable stock
300 g/11 oz arborio rice
150 g/5 oz peas (fresh or frozen)
2.5 ml/½ teaspoon saffron threads
50 g/2 oz freshly grated Parmesan cheese, to serve

Approximately per portion:
2,100 kJ/500 kcal
28 g protein
17 g fat
68 g carbohydrate

- Approximate preparation time: 1 hour 10 minutes

1. Finely chop the onions. Core and seed the peppers and cut the flesh into thin strips.

2. With a sharp knife, cut the veal into 1 cm/½ inch cubes.

3. Heat the olive oil and half the butter in a large saucepan. Add the onions and veal and fry over a medium heat, stirring frequently, until the meat is lightly browned all over. Do not let the onions turn brown. Add the peppers and season with salt and pepper. Stir in 30–45 ml/2–3 tablespoons of the stock, cover and cook over a low heat for about 15 minutes. Meanwhile, bring the remaining stock to the boil.

4. Add the rice to the pan of vegetables and simmer for about 5 minutes, until all the liquid has been absorbed. Pour in 475 ml/16 fl oz of the boiling stock and cook, without covering, over a medium heat, stirring occasionally. Mix in the peas. Cook for about 20 minutes, until the rice is tender and all the liquid has been absorbed. Add more stock while the rice is cooking, if necessary.

5. Just before the end of the cooking time season again with salt and pepper. Stir the saffron into some of the stock and then mix into the rice, together with the remaining butter. Transfer to a warmed serving dish and serve, with the Parmesan cheese.

Risi e verza

RICE WITH SAVOY CABBAGE

Easy to make

Serves 4
1 small Savoy cabbage (about 600 g/1 lb 5 oz)
2 garlic cloves
75 g/3 oz g butter
about 1 litre/1¾ pints meat stock
300 g/11 oz arborio rice
salt
freshly ground black pepper
115 g/4 oz freshly grated Parmesan cheese

Approximately per portion:
2,300 kJ/550 kcal
20 g protein
250g fat
66 g carbohydrate

- Approximate preparation time: 1 hour

1. Cut out the thick cabbage stalks and shred the leaves. Crush the garlic cloves.

2. Melt half the butter in a large saucepan. Add the garlic and fry over a low heat, but do not allow it to turn brown. Add the cabbage and 30–45 ml/2–3 tablespoons of the stock, cover and cook for 10–15 minutes over a low heat, until just tender.

3. Bring the remaining stock to the boil in another pan. Mix the rice into the pan with the cabbage, cook for 2–3 minutes, then pour in 475 ml/16 fl oz of boiling stock.

4. Cook, uncovered, over a medium heat, stirring occasionally, for 20 minutes, until the rice is tender and all the liquid has been absorbed. Add more boiling stock, as necessary.

5. Season to taste with salt and pepper. Before serving mix in the remaining butter and half the cheese. Transfer to a serving dish, serve immediately and hand the remaining cheese separately.

Above: Risi e verza
Below: Risotto alla golosa

Spaghetti alla carbonara

SPAGHETTI WITH BACON AND EGG SAUCE

Easy to make

If unexpected visitors arrive, this pasta dish is quick to prepare and every guest will enjoy it.

Serves 4
salt
400 g/14 oz dried spaghetti
150 g/5 oz pancetta or smoked streaky bacon
1 garlic clove
40 g/1½ oz butter
3 eggs
50 g/2 oz freshly grated pecorino cheese
50 g/2 oz freshly grated Parmesan cheese
freshly ground white pepper

Approximately per portion:
3,600 kJ/860 kcal
31 g protein
51 g fat
68 g carbohydrate

- Approximate preparation time: 30 minutes

1. Bring a large pan of lightly salted water to the boil. Add the spaghetti and cook for about 10 minutes, until just tender, but still firm to the bite. Meanwhile, dice the pancetta or streaky bacon. Crush the garlic.

2. Melt the butter in a large saucepan. Add the garlic and pancetta or bacon and fry until the garlic clove is golden and the bacon is crispy. Remove the garlic from the pan and discard. Cover the pan to keep the pancetta or bacon hot.

3. Beat together the eggs, pecorino cheese and Parmesan cheese and season to taste with salt and white pepper.

4. Drain the spaghetti and mix it into the pan with the pancetta or bacon. Remove the pan from the heat. Pour in the egg and cheese mixture and toss the spaghetti vigorously until all the pasta is coated evenly and the egg has cooked on contact with the hot ingredients. Serve immediately.

Tortellini alla panna

PASTA IN CREAM SAUCE

For guests

You can, of course, also prepare this dish with plain coloured pasta.

Serves 4
1 large onion
6 salad leaves
150 g/5 oz pancetta or smoked streaky bacon
40 g/1½ oz butter
300 g/11 oz peas (fresh or frozen)
salt
freshly ground white pepper
105 ml/7 tablespoons cream
400 g/14 oz fresh coloured tortellini with a meat, spinach or cheese filling
60 ml/4 tablespoons freshly grated Parmesan cheese

Approximately per portion:
3,700 kJ/880 kcal
37 g protein
33 g fat
110 g carbohydrate

- Approximate preparation time: 40 minutes

Tip

If you think ordinary lettuce leaves lack flavour, you can use basil leaves torn into strips instead. And if you like, a hint of garlic would do no harm.

1. Thinly slice the onion and push out into rings. Cut the salad leaves into thin strips. Cut the fat off the pancetta or bacon and chop finely. Dice the lean pancetta or bacon.

2. Melt 15 g/½ oz of the butter in a large saucepan. Add the pancetta fat and fry over a low heat until it has completely melted. Add the onion and fry for about 5 minutes. Add the peas and season to taste with salt and pepper. Pour in half the cream, cover and cook over a low heat until the peas are tender.

3. Meanwhile, bring a large pan of lightly salted water to the boil. Add the tortellini and cook for 8–10 minutes, until just tender, but still firm to the bite.

4. Shortly before the end of the cooking time, stir the remaining butter, the pancetta or bacon, salad leaves and the remaining cream into the pan with the peas. Taste and adjust the seasoning, if necessary, and stir in the cheese. Drain the tortellini, add to the pan and toss to mix well. Transfer to a serving dish and serve immediately.

Pasta al pesto

PASTA WITH BASIL SAUCE

Sophisticated

This is a Ligurian speciality in which home-made trenette are traditionally used, but you can use any long pasta.

Serves 4
200 g/7 oz fresh basil
4 garlic cloves
salt
freshly ground white pepper
30 ml/2 tablespoons pine nuts
75 g/3 oz freshly grated pecorino cheese
200 ml/7 fl oz olive oil
400 g/14 oz dried trenette, linguini or spaghetti

Approximately per portion:
3,800 kJ/900 kcal
19 g protein
60 g fat
73 g carbohydrate

- Approximate preparation time: 45 minutes

1. Pull the basil leaves off the stalks. Crush the garlic.

2. Pound the basil, together with a pinch of salt in a mortar with a pestle. Add a little pepper, the garlic and pine nuts and pound to a paste. Gradually add the cheese and drizzle in the oil very slowly, stirring constantly, until the sauce is smooth and creamy.

3. Meanwhile, bring a large pan of lightly salted water to the boil. Add the pasta and cook for about 10 minutes, until just tender, but still firm to the bite. Drain and reserve a small bowl of the cooking water. Transfer the pasta to a warmed serving dish or bowl.

4. Stir 30 ml/2 tablespoons of the cooking water into the pesto. Add to the spaghetti and toss. Transfer to a warmed serving dish and serve immediately.

Tip

Pesto freezes well, so you can prepare a large quantity at one time and store some for using in the future.

Penne agli asparagi e pomodori

PASTA WITH ASPARAGUS AND TOMATOES

Easy to make

Italian cooks usually use only the tips, that is, the top 10 cm/4 inches of green asparagus spears, when preparing this dish.

Serves 4
1 kg/2¼ lb green asparagus
400 g/14 oz can tomatoes
60 ml/4 tablespoons extra virgin olive oil
salt
freshly ground black pepper
400 g/14 oz dried penne

Approximately per portion:
1,600 kJ/380 kcal
19 g protein
60 g fat
74 g carbohydrate

- Approximate preparation time: 40 minutes

1. Cut off the top 10 cm/4 inches of the asparagus spears, then cut into pieces 3 cm/1¼ inch long. (Cut thicker stalks shorter because they need a longer cooking time).

2. Drain the tomatoes and chop coarsely with a fork.

3. Heat the oil over a low heat in a large saucepan. Add the asparagus and fry for 1 minute, then add the tomatoes. Season to taste with salt and pepper. Cover and cook over a low heat for about 20 minutes, until the vegetables are tender.

4. Meanwhile, bring a large pan of lightly salted water to the boil. Add the penne and cook for about 10 minutes, until just tender, but still firm to the bite. Drain well and transfer to a warmed serving bowl.

5. Add the vegetables to the penne and toss well. Cover and leave to stand for 2–3 minutes before serving.

Above: Penne agli asparagi e pomodori displaying the colours of the Italian flag.
Below: Pasta al pesto is a truly superb pasta dish.

Spaghetti al gorgonzola

SPAGHETTI WITH GORGONZOLA SAUCE

Sophisticated

Bucatini, ditali or penne can also be used to prepare this dish, as all these pastas are hollow on the inside and absorb the creamy cheese sauce well.

Serves 4
salt
400 g/14 oz dried spaghetti
150–200 g/5–7 oz gorgonzola cheese
4 fresh sage leaves
15 g/½ oz butter
250 ml/8 fl oz double cream
freshly ground white pepper

Approximately per portion:
3,200 kJ/760 kcal
25 g protein
43 g fat
69 g carbohydrate

- Approximate preparation time: 30 minutes

1. Bring a large pan of lightly salted water to the boil. Add the spaghetti and cook for about 10 minutes, until just tender, but still firm to the bite.

2. Meanwhile, cut the gorgonzola cheese into small cubes.

3. Melt the butter in a large frying pan. Add the sage and cheese cubes and cook over a low heat until the cheese has melted. Slowly stir in two thirds of the cream. Season to taste with salt and pepper and cook until the sauce has thickened slightly.

4. Drain the spaghetti well and add to the frying pan. Pour over the remaining cream and toss thoroughly. Remove the sage leaves. Transfer to a warm serving dish and serve immediately.

Variation
Spaghetti con gorgonzola e mascarpone
Put 90 g/3½ oz strong gorgonzola, 200 g/7 oz mascarpone, 1 finely chopped onion and 1 celery stick in a food processor or blender and work to form a smooth purée. With the processor switched on, very slowly add sufficient milk to make a thick sauce. Season to taste with salt and a pinch of chilli powder. Heat the sauce in a bain-marie, but do not boil. Toss with the cooked spaghetti and serve.

Spaghetti aglio e olio

SPAGHETTI WITH GARLIC AND OLIVE OIL

Quick

This is a classic, Roman recipe that was originally created as a a dish for the poor, but it has now become fashionable.

Serves 4
salt
400 g/14 oz dried spaghetti
4 garlic cloves
1 bunch fresh parsley
150 ml/¼ pint extra virgin olive oil
1 small piece red chilli

Approximately per portion:
3,000 kJ/10 kcal
15 g protein
43 g fat
68 g carbohydrate

- Approximate preparation time: 20 minutes

1. Bring a large pan of lightly salted water to the boil. Add the spaghetti and cook for about 10 minutes, until just tender, but still firm to the bite.

2. Crush the garlic. Pull the parsley leaves off the stems and chop them finely.

3. Heat the olive oil in a small frying pan over a low heat. Add the garlic, parsley and chilli and fry for about 3 minutes. Season with salt to taste.

4. Drain the spaghetti and transfer to a warmed serving dish. Remove the chilli from the sauce. Mix the sauce together with the spaghetti, tossing thoroughly. Transfer to a warmed serving dish and serve immediately.

The understated sophistication of these two pasta classics is revealed only when you start to eat them.
Above: Spaghetti al gorgonzola
Below: Spaghetti aglio e olio

Lasagne al forno

OVEN-BAKED LASAGNE

For guests

Serves 4
For the meat sauce:
1 onion
1 carrot
1 celery stick
90 g/3½ oz pancetta or smoked streaky bacon
300 g/11 oz mixed minced meat
40 g/1½ oz butter
105 ml/7 tablespoons dry red wine
150 ml/¼ pint meat stock
15 ml/1 tablespoon tomato purée
salt
freshly ground black pepper
1 clove
1 bay leaf
about 150 ml/¼ pint boiling milk

For the béchamel sauce:
50 g/2 oz butter
50 g/2 oz flour
500 ml/17 fl oz milk
salt
freshly ground white pepper

For the pasta:
150 g/5 oz mozzarella cheese
400 g/14 oz lasagne sheets
130 g/4½ oz freshly grated Parmesan cheese
50 g/2 oz butter, plus extra for greasing

Approximately per portion:
5,600 kJ/1,300 kcal
61 g protein
80 g fat
88 g carbohydrate

- Approximate preparation time: 2½ hours

1. First make the meat sauce. Finely chop the onion, carrot and celery. Dice the pancetta or bacon. Mix together the vegetables, pancetta or bacon and minced meat in a bowl.

2. Melt the butter in a large saucepan. Add the meat and vegetable mixture and fry, stirring constantly, until the meat is slightly brown and has broken up. Pour in the red wine, bring to the boil and reduce. Add two thirds of the stock, bring to the boil and reduce.

3. Mix together the tomato purée and the remaining stock and add to the pan. Season to taste with salt and pepper and add the clove and bay leaf. Pour in the milk, cover and simmer over a very low heat for about 1½ hours.

4. To make the béchamel sauce melt the butter in a small saucepan over a low heat. Add the flour and cook, stirring constantly for 2 minutes. Gradually add the milk and bring to the boil, stirring constantly. Simmer until slightly thickened. Season to taste with salt and pepper. Remove the pan from the heat.

5. Drain and dice the mozzarella cheese. Remove the meat sauce from the heat and remove and discard the clove and bay leaf.

6. Bring a large pan of lightly salted water to the boil. Add the lasagne sheets, in batches, and cook for about 10 minutes, until just tender, but still firm to the bite. Place the cooked sheets on a tea cloth. Preheat the oven to 200°C/400°F/ Gas 6. Grease an ovenproof dish with butter.

7. Place a layer of lasagne in the dish. Spoon over enough meat sauce to cover, then spoon over enough béchamel sauce to cover. Top with one third of the mozzarella cheese and sprinkle over one third of the Parmesan cheese. Continue making layers until all the ingredients have been used up, ending with a topping of béchamel sauce and cheese.

8. Dot the top of the lasagne with butter and bake for about 20–30 minutes, until the top is golden brown and bubbling. Serve immediately straight from the dish.

Variation

Pasta alla bolognese

The meat sauce for this lasagne dish is known everywhere in Italy as *ragù alla bolognese* and is very popular. If you do not have time to make a proper lasagne dish, you can simply eat this meat sauce with your favourite pasta. Cook 400 g/ 14 oz dried pasta in a large pan of lightly salted boiling water for about 10 minutes, until tender, but still firm to the bite. Divide the pasta between 4 individual serving plates and pour over the meat sauce. Sprinkle over plenty of freshly grated Parmesan cheese and serve immediately.

Tip

It is quicker to make this dish if you buy ready-to-cook lasagne sheets, which do not have to be boiled first. Make sure that all the lasagne sheets are covered with sauce. If any corners jut out, they will dry out during baking and remain hard.

Melanzane e pomodori al forno

GRATIN OF AUBERGINES AND TOMATOES

Rather time-consuming

Why not bring summer into your home? Even if it is raining outside, the Italian sun rises when you take this typically Mediterranean dish out of the oven!

Serves 4
600 g/1 lb 5 oz aubergines
salt
600 g/1 lb 5 oz ripe beef tomatoes
105 ml/7 tablespoons olive oil
freshly ground black pepper
about 120 ml/4 fl oz sunflower oil
105 ml/7 tablespoons freshly grated Parmesan cheese
30 ml/2 tablespoons fresh white breadcrumbs

Approximately per portion:
2,300 kJ/550 kcal
12 g protein
52 g fat
10 g carbohydrate

- Approximate preparation time: 1¾ hours

1. Cut the aubergines into 1 cm/½ inch thick slices. Put them into a colander in layers, sprinkle salt over each layer and set aside for about 30 minutes to dégorge.

2. Meanwhile, cut the tomatoes into 1 cm/½ inch thick slices. Spread the slices out on kitchen paper in 2 layers. Press the second layer gently against the first with the flat of your hand so that the paper absorbs the liquid.

3. Heat 30 ml/2 tablespoons of the olive oil in a large frying pan. Add the tomatoes and fry for about 30 seconds on each side, then transfer to a dish and season to taste with salt and pepper.

4. Rinse the salt from the aubergines and pat dry with kitchen paper. Heat 30 ml/2 tablespoons sunflower oil in a large frying pan and fry the aubergine slices, in batches, on both sides until golden brown, adding more sunflower oil as necessary. Drain the cooked aubergine slices on kitchen paper.

5. Preheat the oven to 180°C/350°F/Gas 4. Grease an ovenproof dish with 15 ml/1 tablespoon of the remaining olive oil.

6. Arrange the slices of aubergine and tomatoes in the prepared dish in layers, sprinkling each layer generously with Parmesan cheese. Sprinkle the top layer first with cheese and then with breadcrumbs. Drizzle over the remaining olive oil.

7. Bake in the oven for about 30 minutes. Serve immediately.

Variation

Melanzane alla napoletana

Prepare the aubergines as described in the recipe and fry as in step 4. Pull the leaves off the stems of 1 bunch fresh basil and finely chop. Thinly slice 200 g/7 oz mozzarella cheese. Cover the base of an ovenproof dish with fried aubergine slices and cover with half the cheese slices. Season to taste with salt and pepper. Continue making layers in this way until all the ingredients have been used up. Beat 4 eggs with a pinch of salt and pour over the top layer. Bake in the middle of a preheated oven at 180°C/350°F/gas 4 for about 30 minutes.

Tip

This dish looks even more appetizing if you add to its colour by sprinkling the top with finely chopped fresh basil or parsley.

Aubergines prepared in the Italian way taste absolutely irresistible. You really must try Melanzane e pomodori al forno.

Zucchini alla calabrese

COURGETTES WITH BACON AND TOMATOES

Easy to make

Serves 4
600 g/1 lb 5 oz small firm courgettes
500 g/1¼ lb canned tomatoes
200 g/7 oz pancetta or smoked streaky bacon
1 large onion
2 bunches fresh parsley
15 ml/1 tablespoon olive oil
2 garlic cloves
salt
freshly ground black pepper

Approximately per portion:
1,700 kJ/400 kcal
9 g protein
36 g fat
11 g carbohydrate

- Approximate preparation time: 45 minutes

1. Cut the courgettes lengthways into quarters and then cut the quarters crossways into 3 pieces.

2. Drain the tomatoes and reserve the can juice. Coarsely chop the tomatoes.

3. Dice the pancetta or bacon. Thinly slice the onion and push out into rings. Pull the parsley leaves off the stems and chop finely.

4. Heat the oil in a large saucepan. Add the pancetta or bacon cubes and fry until crispy and golden brown. Crush the garlic. Add the onion, garlic and parsley to the saucepan and fry over a low heat for about 10 minutes. Add the tomatoes and courgettes, season to taste with salt and pepper and mix thoroughly.

5. Cover and cook over a very low heat for about 20 minutes, stirring occasionally. Transfer to a warmed serving dish and serve immediately.

Fagiolini in umido

FRENCH BEANS WITH TOMATO AND BASIL

Sophisticated

Serves 4
750 g/1 lb 10 oz French beans
1 large white onion
50 g/2 oz pancetta or smoked streaky bacon
300 g/11 oz beef tomatoes
1 bunch fresh basil
45 ml/3 tablespoons olive oil
salt
freshly ground black pepper

Approximately per portion:
980 kJ/230 kcal
6 g protein
15 g fat
18 g carbohydrate

- Approximate preparation time: 1 hour

1. Cut or break the beans into pieces. Finely chop the onion. Dice the pancetta or bacon into very small cubes.

2. Blanch the tomatoes in boiling water for 1–2 minutes. Drain, skin and cut into quarters. Coarsely chop the quarters.

3. Reserve a few sprigs of basil for the garnish and pull the leaves off the remaining stems. Finely chop the leaves.

4. Heat the oil in a large saucepan. Add the onion and fry over a low heat until soft, but do not let it turn brown. Add the pancetta or bacon, tomatoes and half the chopped basil. Season to taste with salt and pepper. Cover and cook for about 20 minutes. Then stir in the beans and cook over a low heat until they are tender, but still firm to the bite.

5. Season once more with salt and pepper and stir in the remaining chopped basil. Transfer to a warmed serving dish, garnish with the reserved basil sprigs and serve.

Variation
Fagiolini all'acciuge
Cook 50 g/2 oz French beans in lightly salted boiling water until tender, but still firm to the bite. Finely chop 1 garlic clove, the leaves of 1 bunch fresh parsley and 4 anchovies. Melt 15 g/½ oz butter and fry the garlic, parsley and anchovies for 1–2 minutes. Mix in the beans, season with freshly ground black pepper and, if necessary, salt and cook over a low heat for about 5 minutes. Transfer to a warm serving dish and serve immediately.

Above: Zucchini alla calabrese
Below: Fagiolini in umido

Broccoli al prosciutto

BROCCOLI WITH HAM

Serves 4
salt
800 g/1¾ lb broccoli
200 g/7 oz prosciutto (Parma ham), thinly sliced
2 garlic cloves
30 ml/2 tablespoons pork dripping
freshly ground black pepper

Approximately per portion:
1,200 kJ/290 kcal
15 g protein
24 g fat
4 g carbohydrate

- Approximate preparation time: 40 minutes

Variation

Broccoli alle uvette

Soak 15 ml/1 tablespoon sultanas in lukewarm water for about 15 minutes. Drain and squeeze out any excess water. Blanch 750 g/1¾ lb broccoli for about 5 minutes in lightly salted boiling water, then drain. Heat 60 ml/4 tablespoons olive oil in a large frying pan. Add 1 small, finely chopped onion and 1 finely chopped garlic clove and fry over a low heat until soft, but do not allow to become brown. Add the broccoli and 90–135 ml/6–9 tablespoons white wine. Season to taste with salt and pepper. Cover and cook over a low heat until tender, but still firm to the bite. Just before serving, mix in the sultanas.

1. Bring a large pan of lightly salted water to the boil. Trim the broccoli, peel the stems, if necessary, and cut a deep cross into them to ensure that all the parts cook equally. Cook in the boiling water until tender, but still firm to the bite.

2. Remove the broccoli from the pan with a slotted spoon and drain. Meanwhile, cut the ham into thin strips. Chop the garlic.

3. Melt the dripping in a large frying pan. Add the garlic and fry until golden brown, then remove from the pan.

4. Add the ham to the pan and fry over a low heat for 1–2 minutes. Carefully mix in the broccoli, season to taste with salt and pepper, cover and cook over a very low heat for about 5 minutes. Transfer to a warm serving dish and serve immediately.

Funghi al pomodoro

MUSHROOMS WITH TOMATOES

Sophisticated

Serves 4
2 garlic cloves
250 g/9 oz beef tomatoes
75 ml/5 tablespoons olive oil
salt
freshly ground white pepper
5 ml/1 teaspoon dried oregano
500 g/1¼ lb oyster, boletus or button mushrooms

Approximately per portion:
420 kJ/100 kcal
4 g protein
9 g fat
2 g carbohydrate

- Approximate preparation time: 1 hour

Variation

Funghi trifolati

Finely chop 3 garlic cloves. Finely chop the leaves of 1 bunch fresh parsley. Heat 45 ml/3 tablespoons olive oil in a large frying pan. Add 500 g/1¼ lb mushrooms and the garlic and fry over a high heat until all the liquid has evaporated. Mix in the parsley, season to taste with salt and pepper and simmer for a further 5 minutes. Serve either hot or cold.

1. Finely chop the garlic. Blanch the tomatoes in boiling water for 1–2 minutes. Drain, skin and seed, then finely chop the flesh.

2. Heat 30 ml/2 tablespoons of the olive oil in a large saucepan over a low heat. Add the garlic and fry for 1 minute, but do not let it turn brown. Add the tomatoes, season to taste with salt and pepper and add the oregano. Cook over a medium heat for about 20 minutes.

3. Thinly slice the mushrooms. Heat the remaining oil in a large frying-pan. Add the mushrooms and fry over a high heat, stirring occasionally, for about 5 minutes. Season to taste with salt and mix into the tomato sauce.

4. Cover and simmer over a low heat for a further 10 minutes. Serve the mushrooms hot or allow to cool down and serve cold as an antipasto.

Trote alla rustica

TROUT IN A SPICY SAUCE

For guests

As seafood is very expensive, farmed trout is becoming increasingly popular in Italy, too. That the Italians also prepare this fish in a sophisticated way goes without saying.

Serves 4
1 onion
2 carrots
1 celery stick
1 bunch fresh parsley
250 g/9 oz can tomatoes
50 g/2 oz butter
15 ml/1 tablespoon olive oil
2 trout (about 800 g), cleaned
90–135 ml/6–9 tablespoons dry white wine
15 ml/1 tablespoon capers
salt
freshly ground black pepper
1 bay leaf

Approximately per portion:
1,500 kJ/360 kcal
41 g protein
17 g fat
8 g carbohydrate

- Approximate preparation time: 1 hour

1. Finely chop the onion, carrots and celery. Pull the parsley leaves off the stems and finely chop.

2. Drain the tomatoes, then rub through a strainer.

3. Heat 40 g/1½ oz of the butter, together with the oil. in a large frying pan. Add the onion, carrots, celery and parsley and fry over a medium heat, stirring constantly, for about 10 minutes.

4. Add the trout and pour over the wine. Cook over a high heat, frequently spooning the wine over the fish, until the wine has reduced by about half.

5. Finely chop the capers. Season the fish with salt and pepper to taste. Add the bay leaf, capers and tomatoes. Cover and cook over a low heat, spooning the sauce over the fish from time to time, for 15–20 minutes.

6. Transfer the trout to a warmed serving dish and keep warm.

7. Stir the remaining butter into the sauce, then rub the sauce through a strainer. Return to the pan and heat through. Season to taste with salt and pepper. If the sauce is too liquid, reduce over a high heat. Pour the sauce over the fish and serve immediately.

Variation
Trotelle alla menta
Instead of parsley, use 15 ml/1 tablespoon finely chopped fresh basil and 15 ml/1 tablespoon finely chopped fresh mint. Cook half of these with the sauce. Just before serving, mix in the remaining basil, the remaining mint leaves and 15 ml/1 tablespoon butter. Omit the capers and bay leaf.

Tip

Trote alla rustica tastes wonderful with a fresh baguette. Cut the baguette into large chunks in order to soak up the delicious sauce. You could also serve boiled new potatoes with this dish.

Farmed trout, which tends to lack flavour, and frozen trout both work well cooked in this way. Because of the relatively long cooking time over a low heat the flesh takes on an exquisite aroma.

Trote alla rustica – a typically Italian combination of vegetables makes up the 'bed' on which the trout are cooked.

Calamari all'amalfitana

AMALFI-STYLE SQUID

Exclusive

Serves 4
75 g/3 oz sultanas
1 bunch fresh parsley
2 garlic cloves
500 g/1¼ lb can tomatoes
75 g/3 oz pine nuts
75 ml/5 tablespoons olive oil
800 g/1¾ lb prepared squid
120 ml/4 fl oz dry white wine
salt
pinch of chilli powder

Approximately per portion:
1,900 kJ/450 kcal
35 g protein
23 g fat
21 g carbohydrate

- Approximate preparation time: 1¼ hours

1. Put the sultanas into a small bowl, cover with lukewarm water and set aside to soak for about 15 minutes. Drain and squeeze out any excess water.

2. Pull the parsley leaves off the stems and chop finely. Finely chop the garlic. Drain the tomatoes and reserve the can juice. Rub the tomatoes through a strainer. Finely chop the pine nuts.

3. Heat the oil in a large frying pan. Add the garlic and parsley and fry over a low heat for about 5 minutes. Add the squid and cook, stirring occasionally, for about 5 minutes Add the white wine and cook over a high heat until it has reduced. Add the tomatoes and season to taste with salt and chilli powder.

4. Cover and cook over a low heat for about 50 minutes, until the squid is almost tender and cooked through. If the mixture becomes too dry, add a little of the reserved tomato can juice.

5. Mix in the sultanas and the chopped pine nuts and cook over a low heat for a further 10 minutes. Transfer to a warmed serving dish and serve immediately.

Rombo al forno

BAKED HALIBUT

Sophisticated

Serves 4
1 large white onion
1 bunch fresh parsley
½ lemon
50 g/2 oz butter
4 x 250 g/9 oz halibut steaks
salt
freshly ground white pepper
15 ml/1 tablespoon capers
200 ml/7 fl oz double cream
30 ml/2 tablespoons fresh white breadcrumbs

Approximately per portion:
2,100 kJ/500 kcal
49 g protein
31 g fat
10 g carbohydrate

- Approximate preparation time: 1 hour

1. Thinly slice the onion and push out into rings. Pull the parsley leaves off the stems and chop finely. Thinly pare the lemon rind and cut into thin strips.

2. Preheat the oven to 200°C/400°F/Gas 6.

3. Melt 30 ml/2 tablespoons of the butter in a flameproof casserole. Add the onion, cover and cook over a low heat, but do not allow it to turn brown.

4. Add the fish and fry over a medium heat for 1–2 minutes on each side. Season to taste with salt and pepper. Sprinkle over the parsley, lemon rind and capers and pour over the cream.

5. Cover and bake in the oven for about 20 minutes, spooning the sauce over the halibut steaks from time to time.

6. Remove the lid from the casserole. Sprinkle the breadcrumbs over the fish and dot with the remaining butter. Bake until the topping is golden brown. Serve immediately, straight from the casserole.

Above: Rombo al forno
Below: Calamari all'amalfitana

Gamberoni alla caprese

PRAWNS IN A PIQUANT SAUCE

Exclusive

Serves 4
4 garlic cloves
4–5 anchovy fillets
1 bunch fresh flat leaf parsley
400 g/14 oz can tomatoes
90 ml/6 tablespoons olive oil
90–135 ml/6–9 tablespoons dry white wine
salt
pinch of chilli powder
1.5 kg/3½ lb raw prawns
1 lemon, thinly sliced, to garnish
French bread, to serve

Approximately per portion:
2,900 kJ/690 kcal
81 g protein
22 g fat
41 g carbohydrate

- Approximate preparation time: 1 hour

1. Crush the garlic. Chop the anchovy fillets. Pull the parsley leaves off the stems. Reserve a few leaves for the garnish and finely chop the remainder. Drain and chop the tomatoes.

2. Heat the oil in a large saucepan. Add the garlic, anchovies and parsley and fry, stirring occasionally, for about 5 minutes. Add the wine and cook over a high heat, stirring constantly, until it has reduced. Lower the heat, add the tomatoes, season to taste with salt and chilli powder and cook, stirring frequently, until thickened.

3. Add the prawns and simmer over a low heat for about 15 minutes, until they have changed colour and are cooked.

4. Transfer the prawns to 4 individual serving plates. Garnish with the reserved parsley and lemon slices and serve immediately with French bread.

Cozze alla marinara

MUSSELS IN WHITE WINE

Serves 4
2 kg/4½ lb fresh mussels
4 garlic cloves
1 bunch fresh parsley
90 ml/6 tablespoons olive oil
120 ml/4 fl oz dry white wine
2.5 ml/½ teaspoon dried oregano
pinch of chilli powder
salt
4 slices white bread

Approximately per portion:
1,800 kJ/430 kcal
51 g protein
19 g fat
12 g carbohydrate

- Approximate preparation time: 1 hour

1. Scrub the mussels under cold running water and debeard. Discard any that do not shut immediately when sharply tapped.

2. Finely chop 3 of the garlic cloves. Pull the parsley leaves off the stems and chop finely.

3. Heat the oil in a large pan. Add the chopped garlic and half the parsley and fry, stirring frequently over a low heat for about 5 minutes. Add the wine, oregano and chilli powder and season to taste with salt.

4. Add the mussels, cover and cook over a high heat, shaking the pan from time to time, for 5 minutes, or until the shells have opened. Discard any mussels that have not opened.

5. Toast the slices of bread. Cut the remaining garlic clove in half and rub the toast on both sides with the cut surfaces.

6. Ladle the mussels and the cooking liquid into 4 warmed soup bowls. Sprinkle over the remaining parsley and serve with the toasted garlic bread.

Two culinary highlights for fans of sea food: Cozze alla marinara (above) and Gamberoni alla caprese (below).

Merluzzo in umido

COD IN A PIQUANT TOMATO SAUCE

Easy to make

Serves 4
1 onion
2 garlic cloves
1 carrot
1 celery stick
1 bunch fresh parsley
1 bunch fresh basil
1 fresh sage sprig
1 fresh rosemary sprig
500 g/1¼ lb beef tomatoes
1 kg/2¼ lb cod fillet (in one piece)
30–45 ml/2–3 tablespoons flour
60 ml/4 tablespoons olive oil
1 bay leaf
salt
freshly ground white pepper
90–125 ml/6–9 tablespoons dry white wine
boiled new potatoes and green salad, to serve

Approximately per portion:
1,400 kJ/330 kcal
47 g protein
10 g fat
14 g carbohydrate

- Approximate preparation time: 1½ hours

1. Finely chop the onion, garlic, carrot and celery.

2. Pull the parsley, the basil and sage leaves off the stems and chop finely. Pull the rosemary needles off the stems.

3. Blanch the tomatoes in boiling water for 1–2 minutes. Drain, skin, seed and dice the flesh.

4. Coat the fish in the flour and shake off any excess.

5. Heat the oil in a flameproof casserole. Add the onion, garlic, carrot, celery, parsley, basil, sage and rosemary and fry, stirring frequently, for about 5 minutes. Lower the heat, add the tomatoes, cover and cook for about 10 minutes.

6. Preheat the oven to 200°C/ 400°F/Gas 6.

7. Place the fish in the casserole, add the bay leaf, and season to taste with salt and pepper. Bake in the oven for about 30 minutes, occasionally pouring white wine over the fish to prevent its drying out . Halfway through the cooking time, carefully turn the cod over.

8. Remove and discard the bay leaf and serve with boiled new potatoes and a green salad.

Variation

Pesce alle genovese

Finely chop 15 ml/1 tablespoon of soaked and drained dried boletus mushrooms, together with 1 celery stick, the leaves of 1 bunch fresh parsley, 1 carrot, 1 onion, 2 garlic cloves, 3 anchovy fillets, 30 ml/ 2 tablespoons pine nuts and 15 ml/ 1 tablespoon capers. Heat 60 ml/ 4 tablespoons olive oil in a flameproof casserole. Add all the chopped ingredients and fry over a low heat for about 10 minutes. Rub salt and pepper into the fish, coat in flour and place in the casserole. Spoon the fried vegetables and herbs over the fish. Cover and cook in a preheated oven at 180°C/350°F/Gas 4 for about 30 minutes, carefully turning the fish over halfway through the cooking time. Spoon the sauce over the fish from time to time to prevent its drying out. If necessary, add a little vegetable stock.

Tip

If you cannot obtain ripe beef tomatoes, you can use 600 g/1 lb 5 oz canned tomatoes, thoroughly drained and chopped.

Fish have to swim! In this picture the Merluzzo in umido is swimming on a spectacular 'wave' of colourful vegetables, four different herbs and white wine.

Osso buco alla bolognese

VEAL STEW

For guests

Serves 4
1 onion
1 garlic clove
500 g/1¼ lb canned tomatoes
50 g/2 oz butter
4 osso buco veal cutlets (each about 4 cm/1½ inches thick)
salt
freshly ground white pepper
pinch freshly grated nutmeg
pinch ground cloves
90–135 ml/6–9 tablespoons marsala
120 ml/4 fl oz meat stock

Approximately per portion:
1,700 kJ/400 kcal
54 g protein
15 g fat
9 g carbohydrate

- Approximate preparation time: 2¾ hours

1. Finely chop the onion and garlic. Drain and chop the tomatoes.

2. Melt the butter in a large frying pan. Add the onion and garlic and fry over a medium heat for 3–5 minutes, until softened. Add the veal, season to taste with salt, pepper, nutmeg and ground cloves and fry briefly on both sides.

3. Pour in the marsala and cook over a medium heat, turning the meat several times, until the liquid has reduced. Add the tomatoes. Check that the veal is completely covered by the sauce. If not, add some stock. Cover and simmer for about 2 hours over a low heat. Serve immediately.

Variation

Osso buco alla milanese

Thinly slice 1 onion and push out into rings. Melt 50 g/2 oz butter in a frying pan. Add the onion and fry, stirring occasionally, until golden brown. Remove the onion from the frying pan. Lightly flour 4 osso buco veal cutlets and briefly fry on both sides. Add the onion rings, 2 skinned and finely chopped tomatoes and 90–135 ml/6–9 tablespoons white wine. Season to taste with salt and pepper. Simmer over a low heat, turning the veal occasionally. Very finely chop the rind of 1 lemon, 2 anchovy fillets and the leaves of 1 bunch fresh parsley and cook in the sauce for about 10 minutes. Serve immediately.

Fegato di vitello al vino

LIVER IN RED WINE SAUCE

Sophisticated

This dish is traditionally made with calves' liver which has an exceptionally fine texture and a delicate flavour. It may be difficult to obtain – and expensive – so you could substitute lambs' liver.

Serves 4
1 large white onion
75 g/3 oz pancetta or smoked streaky bacon
1 garlic clove
1 bunch fresh parsley
500 g/1¼ lb calves' liver
30 ml/2 tablespoons flour
50 g/2 oz butter
105 ml/7 tablespoons dry red wine
salt
freshly ground black pepper

Approximately per portion:
1,600 kJ/380 kcal
27 g protein
24 g fat
10 g carbohydrate

- Approximate preparation time: 50 minutes

1. Thinly slice the onion and push out into rings. Finely chop the pancetta or bacon and garlic. Pull the parsley leaves off the stems and chop finely.

2. Cut the liver into 5 mm/¼ inch thick slices and lightly dust all over with the flour.

3. Melt the butter in a frying pan over a low heat. Add the garlic, parsley and pancetta or bacon and fry for about 5 minutes. Add the onion rings and fry over a low heat until soft. Pour in the wine and cook over a high heat until almost completely reduced.

4. Add the liver and mix well. Cover and simmer over a low heat for 3–4 minutes. Season to taste with salt and black pepper and serve immediately.

Above: Fegato di vitello al vino
Below: Osso buco alla bolognese

Vitello tonnato

VEAL IN TUNA SAUCE

Exclusive

An aristocratic dish, which is popular not only on hot summer days, but also has a special place as part of a cold buffet. Carving a boned and rolled joint when it is cold prevents it from falling apart.

Serves 4
2 carrots
2 celery sticks
1 onion.
750 g/1 lb 10 oz loin or leg of veal, boned
2 bay leaves
2 cloves
approximately 1 litre/1¾ pints dry white wine
salt
freshly ground white pepper
fresh parsley sprigs and lemon slices, to garnish

For the sauce:
150 g/5 oz can tuna fish in oil, drained
3–4 anchovy fillets
50 g/2 oz capers
50 g/2 oz gherkins
2 egg yolks
juice of 1 lemon
120 ml/4 fl oz extra virgin olive oil

Approximately per portion:
2,200 kJ/520 kcal
53 g protein
31 g fat
6 g carbohydrate

- Approximate preparation time: 18¾–19¾ hours

1. Thinly slice the carrots, celery and onion. Put the veal into a large dish, together with the carrots, celery, onion, bay leaves and cloves. Pour over the white wine. Cover and set aside in the refrigerator to marinate overnight.

2. The next day, roll the meat tightly in a piece of muslin tied with string so that it retains its shape during cooking.

3. Put the veal into a large saucepan. Bring the marinade to the boil in another saucepan and pour it over the veal. The meat should be well covered, so add some extra boiling water, if necessary. Season to taste with salt and pepper.

4. Cover and simmer over a low heat for about 1½ hours, until the meat is thoroughly cooked, but still firm. Set the cooking liquid aside to cool completely.

5. Meanwhile, finely chop the tuna, anchovies, capers and gherkins.

6. Beat together the egg yolks and lemon juice with a hand whisk until frothy. Beat in the oil, drop by drop, until creamy.

7. Stir in the tuna, anchovies, capers and gherkins. Stir in sufficient cooled cooking liquid to give the consistency of double cream. Season to taste with salt and white pepper.

8. Unwrap the veal, pat dry with kitchen paper and cut into slices about 3 mm/⅛ inch thick with a sharp knife. Arrange the veal on a plate so that the slices overlap.

9. Thoroughly stir the sauce again, then pour evenly over the meat. Cover the dish with clear film and set aside in a cool place for 5–6 hours.

10. Serve the veal garnished with the parsley sprigs and lemon slices.

Tip

If there is not enough time to marinate the veal first, you can cook it straight away with the other ingredients and the wine. In which case, it is satisfactory to chop the vegetables coarsely.

Vitello tonnato is an absolute must for gourmets! Anyone who has not eaten it before really should try it.

Agnello alla reggiana

MARINATED LAMB

Easy to make

The marinade makes the meat tender and gives it a more delicate and subtle flavour.

Serves 4
1 kg/2¼ lb boneless shoulder of lamb
2 garlic cloves
10 juniper berries
5 ml/1 teaspoon fresh rosemary needles
5 fresh sage leaves
90 ml/6 tablespoons olive oil
juice of 1 lemon
15 ml/1 tablespoon tarragon vinegar
salt
freshly ground black pepper
120 ml/4 fl oz dry white wine

Approximately per portion:
3,000 kJ/710 kcal
45 g protein
57 g fat
2 g carbohydrate

- Approximate preparation time: 4½ hours

1. Cut the lamb into 1 cm/½ inch cubes and place in a large dish. Crush together the garlic and juniper berries, then mix together with the rosemary, sage, olive oil, lemon juice and tarragon vinegar. Season to taste with salt and pepper and pour over the lamb. Turn and stir the lamb to ensure that it is thoroughly coated.

2. Set the lamb aside in the refrigerator to marinate for at least 3 hours, stirring it frequently.

3. Preheat the oven to 180°C/350°F/Gas 4. Transfer the lamb and the marinade to a casserole. Cover and cook the oven for about 45 minutes.

4. Add the wine and cook until almost no liquid remains in the casserole and the meat is slightly brown. Serve immediately.

Scaloppine di maiale al marsala

PORK ESCALOPES IN MARSALA SAUCE

For guests

Serves 4
20 g/¾ oz pancetta or smoked streaky bacon
2 garlic cloves
30 ml/2 tablespoons olive oil
8 pork escalopes (about 500 g/1¼ lb)
sal
freshly ground black pepper
30–45 ml/2–3 tablespoons flour
90–135 ml/6–9 tablespoons marsala
30 ml/2 tablespoons meat stock

Approximately per portion:
1,200 kJ/290 kcal
26 g protein
17 g fat
2 g carbohydrate

- Approximate preparation time: 40 minutes

1. Finely dice the pancetta or bacon. Crush the garlic.

2. Heat the oil in a large frying pan over a moderately high heat. Add the pancetta or bacon and garlic and fry until the garlic is golden brown. Remove the garlic from the pan.

3. Meanwhile, season the pork with salt and pepper and lightly dust with the flour.

4. Add the escalopes to the pan and fry for 1–2 minutes on each side until they are lightly browned. Pour in the marsala and bring to the boil. Cook, turning once, for 5–7 minutes, until cooked through. Transfer the pork to a warmed serving dish.

5. Add the stock to the frying pan and heat, stirring, until slightly thickened. Pour the sauce over the escalopes and serve immediately.

Above: Agnello alla reggiana
Below: Scaloppine di maiale al marsala

Coniglio alla piacentina

RABBIT WITH WINE AND NUTS

Exclusive

Gremolata, a mixture of finely chopped herbs, lemon rind and crushed garlic, is typically Italian. The recipe here has an extra addition of chopped walnuts. You can cook them briefly with the other ingredients or sprinkle them over the finished dish.

Serves 4
3–4 ripe beef tomatoes
75 g/3 oz pancetta or smoked streaky bacon
45 ml/3 tablespoons olive oil
8–10 rabbit portions
250 ml/8 fl oz dry white wine
salt
freshly ground black pepper
1 bunch fresh parsley
1 fresh rosemary sprig
½ small lemon
1 garlic clove
8–10 shelled walnuts
crusty white bread or polenta and green salad, to serve

Approximately per portion:
5,500 kJ/1,300 kcal
140 g protein
77 g fat
9 g carbohydrate

- Approximate preparation time: 1¾ hours

1. Blanch the tomatoes in boiling water for 1–2 minutes. Drain, skin, seed and finely chop the flesh.

2. Finely dice the pancetta or smoked streaky bacon.

3. Heat the oil in a saucepan. Add the pancetta or bacon and fry for 1 minute. Add the rabbit portions and fry over a medium heat, turning frequently, until golden brown all over.

4. Pour in the wine and cook, turning the rabbit portions several times, until the liquid has reduced by half. Season the rabbit with salt and pepper to taste. Add the chopped tomatoes, cover and cook over a low heat for about 35 minutes.

5. Meanwhile, pull the parsley leaves off the stems and finely chop. Pluck off the needles from the rosemary sprig. Thinly pare the lemon rind and finely chop.

6. Crush the garlic. Finely chop the walnut kernels with a large knife or a kitchen cleaver.

7. Mix together the parsley, rosemary, lemon rind, garlic and walnuts. Stir this gremolata into the saucepan, cover and simmer over a low heat for about 10 minutes, or until the rabbit is tender and cooked through.

8. Arrange the cooked rabbit portions and the sauce on a deep serving dish and serve immediately with white bread or polenta and a green salad.

Variation

Coniglio in umido

Heat 15 g/½ oz butter and 45 ml/3 tablespoons olive oil in a large saucepan. Fry 8–10 rabbit portions, turning frequently, until golden brown all over. Add 2 crushed garlic cloves, 5 ml/1 teaspoon rosemary needles, 4 chopped fresh sage leaves and 1 bay leaf and fry for about 5 minutes. Season to taste with salt, pepper and nutmeg. Pour in 120 ml/4 fl oz red wine and reduce. Rub 500 g/1¼ lb skinned tomatoes through a strainer and add to the saucepan, together with 45 ml/3 tablespoons pine nuts. Cover and cook over a low heat for about 45 minutes, or until the rabbit is tender and completely cooked through.

What makes this festive rabbit dish so special is the gremolata, an aromatic mixture of chopped herbs, lemon rind, garlic and nuts.

Macedonia allo zabaione

FRUIT SALAD WITH MARSALA SAUCE

Easy to make

Serves 4
2 yellow peaches
6–8 apricots
1 firm ripe pear
1 apple
90 g/3½ oz raspberries
90 g/3½ oz wild strawberries
juice of 1 lemon
90 g/3½ oz caster sugar
3 egg yolks
120 ml/4 fl oz marsala

Approximately per portion:
660 kJ/160 kcal
4 g protein
6 g fat
22 g carbohydrate

- Approximate preparation time: 1½ hours

Variation

You can vary the flavours of zabaione according to your own taste by using dry white wine instead of marsala or by using half marsala and half wine. You can also add the grated rind of a lemon or orange or an aromatic liqueur.

1. Peel the peaches, cut them in half, remove the stones and cut the flesh into cubes. Cut the apricots in half, remove the stones and cut the flesh into slices. Peel and core the pear and apple and cut into cubes.

2. Put the peaches, apricots, pear, apple, raspberries and strawberries into a bowl and mix in the lemon juice and about 50 g/2 oz of the sugar. Set aside in the refrigerator for about 1 hour, turn the pieces of fruit and the berries carefully once.

3. Meanwhile, in a heatproof bowl beat together the egg yolks and the remaining sugar with a whisk or hand-held beater until creamy. Then set the bowl on a saucepan of hot, but not boiling, water. Do not allow the base of the bowl to touch the surface of the water. Slowly beat in the marsala and continue beating until thickened and creamy.

4. Transfer the bowl to a container of iced water and stir until the sauce has cooled to lukewarm. Divide the fruit salad between 4 individual serving bowls. Pour the sauce over the fruit salad or hand separately.

Torta al mascarpone

MASCARPONE GÂTEAU

For guests

Makes 26 cm/10¼ inch cake
90 g/3½ oz plain chocolate
26 cm/10¼ inch cooked and cooled sponge cake (recipe on page 58)
120 ml/4 fl oz lightly sugared black coffee
200 ml/7 fl oz rum
3 eggs
75 g/3 oz caster sugar
375 g/12 oz mascarpone cheese

Approximately per slice:
1,400 kJ/330 kcal
14 g protein
15 g fat
37 g carbohydrate

- Approximate preparation time: 8½ hours

Variation

Tiramisu

Prepare the cream topping using 3 egg yolks, 50 g/2 oz caster sugar, 250 g/9 oz mascarpone cheese and 3 stiffly whisked egg whites. Cut the sponge into 8 pieces and carefully dip each piece into a mixture of 120 ml/4 fl oz cold black coffee and 200 ml/7 fl oz rum, making sure that the sponge is moist, but still firm. Cover the bottom of a dish with 4 sponges. Spread half the cream topping over the sponge layer. Repeat this process with the remaining sponges and cream topping. Chill in the refrigerator for 8 hours. Before serving, sprinkle cocoa powder over the top.

1. Grate the chocolate. Cut through the prepared sponge cake twice horizontally to make three even layers. Sprinkle the coffee and rum over the three sponge layers.

2. Separate the eggs. Beat together the yolks with the sugar until thickened. Beat in the mascarpone cheese, a little at a time, and continue beating until thick and smooth. Whisk the egg whites until stiff, then fold them into the egg yolk mixture.

3. Place one layer of the sponge cake on a serving plate. Spread one third of the creamy topping over it and sprinkle one third of the grated chocolate on top. Top with another layer of sponge cake and repeat this process twice until a three-layered gâteau has been formed. The topmost layer will have a topping of the cream covered with grated chocolate.

4. Chill in the refrigerator. It is best to allow the cake to cool overnight, as the gâteau should be served very cold.

Cassata

SICILIAN DESSERT

Exclusive

Serves 4
6 eggs
185 g/6½ oz icing sugar
15 g/½ oz vanilla sugar
90 g/3½ oz self-raising flour
75 g/3 oz cornflour

For the filling:
200 g/7 oz mixed candied fruit
75 g/3 oz plain chocolate
500 g/1¼ lb ricotta cheese
185 g/6½ oz caster sugar
15 g/1½ oz vanilla sugar
600 ml/1 pint maraschino liqueur or rum (optional)
300 ml/½ pint double cream, glacé cherries, candied fruits, slivered almonds or chocolate sprinkles, to decorate

Approximately per portion:
6,700 kJ/1,600 kcal
38 g protein
74 g fat
180 g carbohydrate

- Approximate preparation time: 11½–12½ hours

1. Line a 26 cm/10¼ inch springform tin with non-stick baking paper. Preheat the oven to 180°C/350°F/Gas 4.

2. First make the cake. Separate the eggs and beat together the yolks, icing sugar and vanilla sugar until frothy. Whisk the egg whites until stiff, then fold into the egg yolk mixture. Sift over the flour and cornflour and fold in. Pour the cake batter into the springform tin and smooth out the top. Bake in the oven for 30–35 minutes. Test with a skewer to see if it is cooked through. Set the sponge aside for about 6 hours to cool completely.

3. To make the filling, dice the candied fruit and chocolate. Mix together the ricotta cheese, sugar, vanilla sugar and 400 ml/14 fl oz of the liqueur or rum to form a smooth paste. Stir in the candied fruit and chocolate.

4. Cut the sponge into 1 cm/½ inch wide strips and line the base and sides of a bowl or loaf tin with some of the strips. Fill evenly with the cream mixture, smooth the top and cover with the remaining sponge.

5. Drizzle over the remaining liqueur or rum and chill in the refrigerator for 4–5 hours.

6. Carefully turn the cake out of bowl or tin on to a serving plate. Stiffly whip the cream and use to coat the top and sides of the cake. Decorate with glacé cherries, candied fruit, slivered almonds or chocolate sprinkles, as desired.

Amaretti

LITTLE MACAROONS

Amaretti are made with apricot kernels, but as these can be difficult to obtain, this recipe uses almonds.

Makes about 90
300 g/11 oz shelled almonds
300 g/11 oz sugar
2–3 egg whites
icing sugar, for dusting

Approximately per biscuit:
145 kJ/35 kcal
1 g protein
2g fat
4 g carbohydrate

- Approximate preparation time: 1½ hours

1. Blanch the almonds in boiling water for 2–3 minutes, drain, remove the skin and dry well. (This is best done by heating in the oven at the lowest setting.)

2. Finely crush the almonds with the sugar in a mortar with a pestle. Alternatively, finely chop with a kitchen cleaver, then mix them in a bowl with the rest of the sugar. If you have to do this in batches, match the weights of almonds and sugar in each batch.

3. Lightly beat the egg whites, then gradually mix enough egg white into the almond mixture to form a firm dough.

4. Preheat the oven to 120°C/250°F/Gas ½. Line a baking sheet with kitchen foil. Place nut-sized portions of the mixture on the foil spacing them well apart. Dust with icing sugar and bake in the oven for about 30 minutes. Set aside to cool completely.

Above: Cassata
Below: Amaretti

Zuppa inglese

TRIFLE

For guests

Serves 4
500 ml/17 fl oz milk
5 eggs
150 g/5 oz caster sugar
150 g/5 oz mixed candied fruit
26 cm/10¼ inch cooked and cooled sponge cake (recipe on page 58)
50 ml/2 fl oz rum
50 ml/2 fl oz amaretto liqueur
15 ml/1 tablespoon icing sugar

Approximately per portion:
5,000 kJ/1,200 kcal
43 g protein
37 g fat
170 g carbohydrate

- Approximate preparation time: 1 hour 5 minutes

1. Bring the milk to the boil in a saucepan, remove from the heat and set aside to cool slightly.

2. Separate 3 of the eggs. In a bowl beat together the 2 whole eggs, the egg yolks and sugar until thick creamy. Gradually pour in the milk, beating constantly.

3. Tip the custard mixture into a clean pan and set over a low heat. Bring to just below boiling point, stirring constantly, but do not allow to boil. Pour the custard into a bowl and set aside to cool completely, stirring from time to time to prevent a skin forming.

4. Dice the candied fruit and mix it into the custard.

5. Using a sharp knife, cut the sponge cake into strips about 1 cm/½ inch wide. Cover the base of an ovenproof dish with some of the strips of sponge.

6. Carefully sprinkle a little rum over the sponge strips and cover with a layer of custard and sprinkle with a little amaretto. Top with more sponge strips and repeat this process until all the ingredients have been used up, ending with a layer of sponge strips.

7. Preheat the oven to 240°C/475°F/Gas 9.

8. Whisk together the egg whites and icing sugar to form soft peaks. Spoon the meringue into a piping bag and use to decorate the gâteau.

9. Bake in the oven until the meringue topping has turned light golden brown.

Variation
You can cover the trifle with stiffly whipped double cream, instead of meringue topping. In which, case, do not bake in the oven.

Crema di mascarpone agli amaretti

MASCARPONE CREAM WITH AMARETTI

Quick

Serves 4
90 g/3½ oz amaretti
45 ml/3 tablespoons amaretto liqueur
4 eggs
50 g/2 oz caster sugar
200 g/7 oz mascarpone cheese
4 glacé cherries, to decorate

Approximately per portion:
2,300 kJ/550 kcal
23 g protein
30 g fat
46 g carbohydrate

- Approximate preparation time: 1 hour 20 minutes

1. Put the amaretti in a plastic bag and crush with a rolling pin. Transfer the crumbs to a small bowl and add the liqueur.

2. Separate the eggs. Beat together the egg yolks and the sugar to form a thick, creamy mixture. Fold in the mascarpone cheese and the soaked amaretti crumbs and mix gently.

3. Whisk the egg whites stiffly and fold into the mascarpone mixture. Spoon the mixture into 4 sundae dishes or tall glasses.

4. Decorate each one with a glacé cherry and chill in the refrigerator for at least 1 hour before serving.

No one with a sweet tooth can resist these desserts!
Above: Crema di mascarpone agli amaretti.
Below: Zuppa inglese

RECIPES AND INDEX

P

R

S

T

V

Z

Great Little Cook Books

Italian Cooking

Published originally under the title *Italienisch kochen* by Gräfe und Unzer Verlag GmbH, München

English-language edition

This edition published by
Aura Books plc

Translation:
Translate-A-Book, Oxford

Editing:
Linda Doeser

Typesetting:
Organ Graphic, Abingdon

10 9 8 7 6 5 4 3 2 1
Printed in Dubai

ISBN 1 901683 51 6

Note:
Quantities for all recipes are given in both metric and imperial measures and, if appropriate, in standard measuring spoons. They are not interchangeable, so readers should follow one set or the other.
5 ml = 1 teaspoon
15 ml = 1 tablespoon

Odette Teubner
was taught by her father, the internationally renowned food photographer, Christian Teubner. After that she worked for some months as a fashion photographer. She now works exclusively in the Teubner Studio for Food Photography. In her spare time she is an enthusiastic painter of children's portraits, using her own son as a model.

Kerstin Mosny
studied photography at a college in French-speaking Switzerland. She then worked as an assistant to various photographers, including the food photographer, Jürgen Tapprich, in Zurich. She now works in the Teubner Photography Studio.

Marieluise Christl-Licosa
was born and grew up in the Tyrol. For many years she lived in Milan, together with her husband and their four sons, and it was there that she mastered the Italian language and studied Italian cuisine at its source. Numerous trips and long visits to all parts of Italy led to many lasting international friendships. With real passion, Mrs Christl-Licosa collected recipes from Piedmontese mountain farmers, from cooks in aristocratic villas in Lombardy and Tuscany and, by no means least, from the head chefs of well-known restaurants in major cities. Since then, her work in the kitchen has become her hobby. She is currently teaching Italian at an adult education institute and holds weekend seminars in Italian cuisine.